SHARK Snacks

Chicago, Illinois

Printed and bound in the United States by
Lake Book Manufacturing, Inc

10 09 08 07 06
10 9 8 7 6 5 4 3 2 1

Library of Congress Cataloging-in-Publication Data
Spilsbury, Louise.
  Shark snacks : food chains and webs / Louise and Richard Spilsbury.
     p. cm.
  Includes bibliographical references.
  ISBN 1-4109-1942-0 (library binding) -- ISBN 1-4109-1973-0 (pbk.)
  1. Food chains (Ecology)--Juvenile literature. 2. Sharks--Food--Juvenile literature. I. Spilsbury, Richard. II. Title.
   QH541.14.S6826 2004
   577'.16--dc22
                                              2005009546

Acknowledgments
The author and publishers are grateful to the following for permission to reproduce copyright material: Chris Fallows pp. 22–23; Corbis pp. 12–13 (Brownie Harris), 16–17 (Brandon D. Cole), 20 (Royalty-free); FLPA/Minden Pictures pp. 18 (Norbert Wu), 6–7 (Mike Parry); Naturepl.com pp. 17 inset (Jeff Rottman), 19 (Brandon Cole), 27 (Doc White); Oceanwide Images pp. 20–21 (Gary Bell), 4–5 (Gary Bell); Oxford Scientific Films pp. 14–15 (Dave Fleetham), 20–21 (Dave Fleetham), 24–25 (Carl Roessler); Photovault p. 10 (Wernher Krutein); Science Photo Library pp. 8–9 (Andrew Syred).

Cover photograph of a great white shark, reproduced with permission of Corbis (Amos Nachoum).

Illustrations by Bigtop.

The publishers would like to thank Nancy Harris and Harold Pratt for their assistance in the preparation of this book.

Every effort has been made to contact copyright holders of any material reproduced in this book. Any omissions will be rectified in subsequent printings if notice is given to the publishers.

The paper used to print this book comes from sustainable resources.

Disclaimer
All the Internet addresses (URLs) given in this book were valid at the time of going to press. However, due to the dynamic nature of the Internet, some addresses may have changed, or sites may have changed or ceased to exist since publication. While the author and publishers regret any inconvenience this may cause readers, no responsibility for any such changes can be accepted by either the author or the publishers.

Contents

Some words are printed in bold, **like this**. You can find out what they mean on page 30. You can also look in the box at the bottom of the page where they first appear.

Shark Snacks

There is a rumble in the ocean. The great white shark is hungry. It needs to eat and it is looking for a snack.

All animals need to eat. If you are hungry, you might eat an apple. But the great white shark is a **carnivore**. A carnivore eats only meat. The shark eats raw meat from the animals it hunts.

Get out of the way! The great white ▶ shark is ready to sink its razor-sharp teeth into some flesh.

What's in a name?

The great white shark is huge and has a white belly. That's why it's called a great white shark! It also has a huge mouth. The mouth is full of teeth. The teeth are so sharp they can slice through skin, flesh, and bone.

carnivore   animal that eats only meat

Ruler of the ocean

The great white shark rules all the fish in the ocean. It is not afraid of anything. The great white shark is a **predator**. It hunts and eats other animals.

The animals that a predator eats are called its **prey**. The great white shark's prey include tuna, squid, and dolphins. A sea lion is also one of the shark's favorite snacks.

6

energy	ability to make a change happen
food chain	series of living things that eat one another
predator	animal that eats other animals
prey	animal that gets eaten by other animals

The sea lion is a predator, too. The sea lion gets **energy** by eating fish. All living things need energy to stay alive. Energy is the ability to make a change happen. Energy allows living things to move, hunt, and survive. Fish are also predators. They get energy by eating even smaller animals.

The animals that eat each other form a **food chain**. A food chain shows how energy passes from one living thing to another. So, where does this chain begin?

The great white shark is at ▼ the end of this food chain.

Great white shark

?

?

?

?

?

The start of the chain

This **food chain** begins with the tiny things in this photo. They are **plankton**. They live on the surface of the oceans.

The living things in plankton are very tiny. You can only see them through a microscope. Plankton is the start of the ocean food chain. The great white shark wouldn't exist without plankton.

Plankton is made up of tiny **algae** and tiny animals. Algae are like plants. Algae do not eat other things. They use **energy** from the Sun to make food inside their bodies. This means they are **producers**. An animal that eats plankton gets some of this energy.

This is a drop of ocean ▶ water seen through a microscope. The strange shapes are plankton.

algae   plant-like living things
plankton   tiny algae and animals that live in the oceans
producer   living thing that makes its own food

Great white shark

?

?

?

?

Algae are producers. ▶
They use energy from
the Sun to make food.

Plankton

Home Delivery

Mussels are the couch potatoes of the ocean world. They stick to one rock for most of their lives. They don't bother to look for food. They wait for a home delivery of fresh **plankton**.

▼ Ordering in! A mussel sticks to a rock. It waits for the water to deliver its dinner.

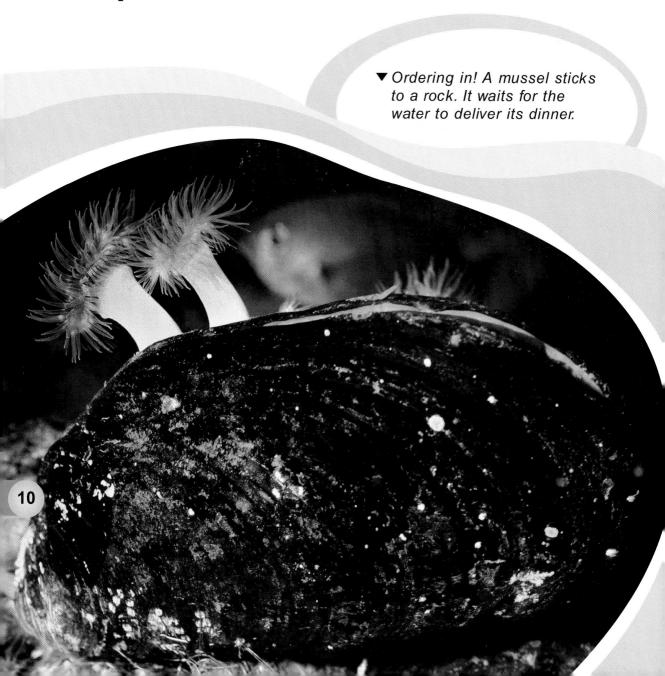

A mussel is a **consumer**. A consumer is an animal that eats other living things. A mussel sticks two tubes out of its shells when it wants to eat. The mussel sucks seawater in through one tube. There are slimy threads inside the mussel's shells. The threads catch the plankton in the water. Then, the mussel spits the water out through the other tube.

A mussel closes its shells tightly after eating. The shells should protect the mussel's soft body from many ocean **predators**.

Very thirsty!

Mussels suck in and squirt out 0.7 gallons (3 liters) of water every hour.

Great white shark

?

?

?

The mussel is the second link in this **food chain**. ▶

Mussel

Plankton

consumer living thing that eats other living things

Handle with care

The spiny lobster hides in rocks during the day. At night it comes out and crawls across the ocean floor. The lobster waves its long feelers, called antennae. The antennae reach out from the lobster's head. They sense movement and sniff out food.

Tonight, the antennae pick up the smell of mussels. The smell is like a message saying "Dinner is served!"

The spiny lobster moves in for the kill. It stands over its **prey.** Then it clamps its jaws tightly around the mussel's shells. It bites down hard. There is a crunching sound. The lobster breaks off chunks and eats them.

Eat up!

A lobster's teeth are in its stomach. That's where it grinds up its food — shells, flesh, and all.

The spikes on the ▶ spiny lobster's shell are very sharp. They would slice your hand if you tried to grab it!

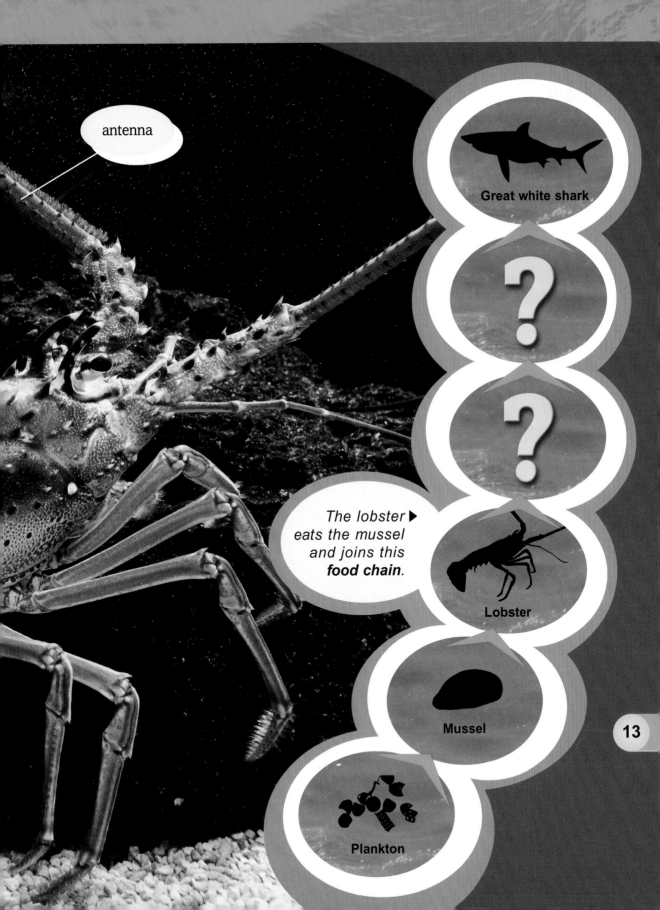

antenna

Great white shark

?

?

The lobster ▶
eats the mussel
and joins this
food chain.

Lobster

Mussel

Plankton

13

No escape

There is an octopus in the dark water above the spiny lobster. The octopus drops down quietly and quickly. It gets closer to the lobster. The octopus stretches out its long tentacles very wide.

At the last moment the lobster senses the danger. It flicks its tail to escape. Too late! The octopus wraps its tentacles around the lobster. The tentacles drag the lobster towards the open mouth of the octopus.
The lobster has now become lunch.

There are more than 200 suckers on each tentacle. The suckers act like sticky fingers. They grip the **prey** tightly.

Kiss of death!

The spit of an octopus is poisonous. The poison is strong enough to knock out prey. It also makes the prey's flesh soft for the octopus to swallow.

Great white shark

?

The octopus ▶
comes next in
*this **food chain**.*

Octopus

Lobster

The octopus has
a hard, sharp beak inside its
mouth. It uses this beak to
chop up food.

Mussel

Plankton

Master of disguise

The octopus feels full after its lobster lunch. However, this is no time to relax. The octopus may be a good **predator**, but it is **prey** for a lot of other animals. An octopus has some clever tricks to make sure it is not eaten.

An octopus changes color when it needs to hide quickly. Its skin turns lighter or darker to match the sand or rock nearby. This clever **camouflage** means that other animals cannot see the octopus. It just disappears from sight.

camouflage   color or pattern that helps an animal blend into the background

▲ *A cloud of ink gives the octopus a chance to make a quick getaway.*

If a predator does spot it, the octopus squirts out a cloud of ink. The octopus ink floats in the water behind the octopus. It confuses predators. This gives the octopus a chance to make a quick getaway. Yet it doesn't always work . . .

Sea Lion Dinner

The sea lion bursts through the dark water. It stretches its neck forward. It bites into the octopus. The octopus swipes at the sea lion with its tentacles. The octopus is **prey** now. Soon, the octopus is history!

Sea lions search the ocean floor for food. It is too dark to see, so sea lions listen for noises. The noises tell them that prey is near.

Sea lions have whiskers on their faces. The whiskers can feel slight ripples in the water. The ripples tell the sea lion that an animal is moving nearby.

whiskers

▲ A sea lion has tough, sharp teeth like all **carnivores**. The teeth grip and crush the sea lion's prey.

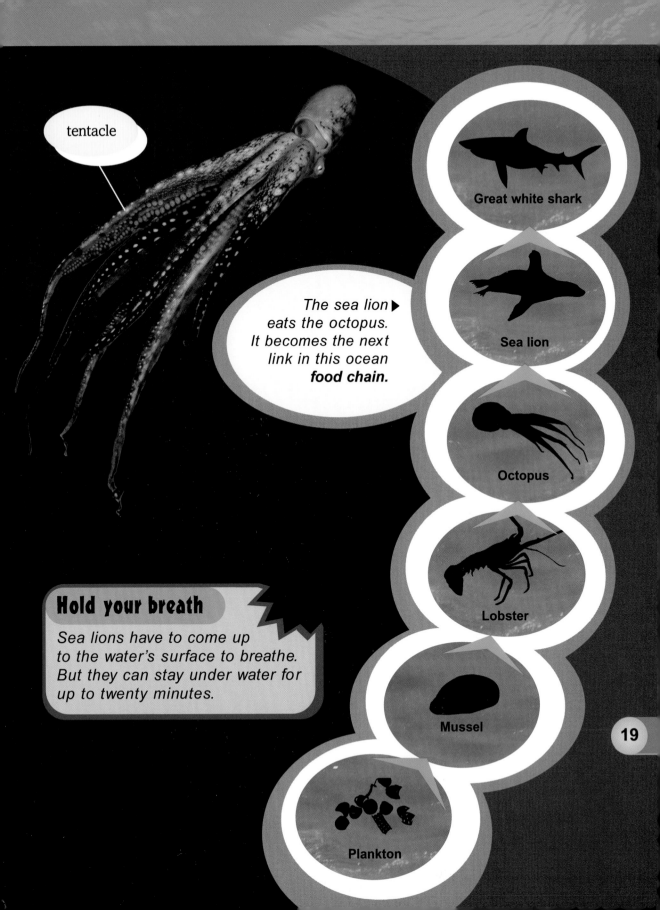

tentacle

The sea lion ▶ eats the octopus. It becomes the next link in this ocean **food chain.**

Hold your breath

Sea lions have to come up to the water's surface to breathe. But they can stay under water for up to twenty minutes.

Great white shark

Sea lion

Octopus

Lobster

Mussel

Plankton

Ocean acrobats

Sea lions look out for danger when they dive for food. They are not as big or as strong as other **predators** such as sharks. But sea lions are the acrobats of the ocean. Sea lions can quickly change direction. They can spin and twist around. They can even leap high out of the water.

Sea lions have ▼ strong front flippers.

They push their flippers ▲ up and down against the water to move forward.

flippers

▲ Sea lions can paddle fast through the water using their flippers.

Sea lions usually hang around in groups. They bark to warn each other when danger is near. Then, they leap onto rocks when they are near land. It is safer than being in the water.

However, what happens if a sea lion is out at sea and all alone? What happens if it doesn't notice the shark swimming beneath it?

Shark Attack

The great white shark flicks its tail. It shoots up through the water. It opens its mouth just before reaching the surface . . .

The shark is the ▶ final **consumer** in this **food chain**.

Great white shark

The shark slams into its **prey** with a thud. Then, the shark leaps out of the water. It holds the shocked sea lion tightly in its jaws.

A sea lion makes an **energy**-filled shark snack. A great white shark feels full for a couple of weeks after eating a sea lion.

Sea lion

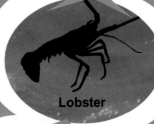

Octopus

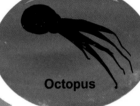

Lobster

See the difference?

Great white sharks sometimes attack surfers when they paddle out to sea on their surfboards. From below, the shape of a surfboard looks like a sea lion.

Mussel

Plankton

Built to eat

The great white shark is a top **predator**.
Check out its deadly design!

The back **fin** keeps a shark straight up in the water.

The side fins help the shark to steer, and help to stop it from sinking.

The shark moves its tail fin from side to side as it moves through the water.

A shark swims non-stop. It uses **gills** to breathe under water.

Sharks can smell blood from long distances.

The front rows of teeth bite and rip. The back rows are new teeth.

25

fin stiff, flat flap of skin that fish use to swim
gills body parts that allow fish to breathe under water

When a shark becomes a snack...

When a shark dies, it sinks to the ocean floor. Its body disappears within a few months.

The dead shark is eaten away. Animals such as fish and crabs come first. They nibble off chunks of flesh. They leave large holes in the shark's side.

Then **bacteria** join the feast. Bacteria are living things. They are so small you cannot see them. Bacteria are **decomposers**. They break down the shark's body into chemicals.

As bacteria feed, they release food into the sea. **Plankton** use this food to help them grow. This brings the **food chain** back to where we started.

bacteria   tiny living things
decomposer   living thing that breaks down dead bodies

Only the teeth and bones of the shark are left once bacteria get to work.

Shark in a web

A great white shark doesn't just eat sea lions. It might eat fish such as herring, too.

The great white shark is part of more than one **food chain**. It is part of a **food web**. A food web shows how food chains in a particular place link to one another.

Killer whale

Tuna

Herring

*This food web shows ▶ how ocean food chains are linked. The arrows show how **energy** flows from one animal to another.*

Glossary

algae plantlike living things. Some algae are part of plankton. Some are seaweed.

bacteria tiny living things. Some bacteria break down (decompose) dead plants and animals.

camouflage color or pattern that helps an animal blend into the background. An octopus can make its skin color lighter or darker to help it hide.

carnivore animal that eats only meat. A great white shark is a carnivore.

consumer living thing that eats other living things. Great white sharks are consumers because they eat sea lions and other animals.

decomposer living thing that breaks down dead bodies. Bacteria are decomposers.

energy ability to make a change happen. Animals get energy from eating plants or other animals.

fin stiff, flat flap of skin. Fish use fins to swim and steer.

food chain series of living things that eat one another. A food chain diagram shows how energy flows from one living thing to another.

food web diagram showing how food chains are linked to one another

gills body parts that allow fish to breathe under water. Sharks have gills.

plankton tiny algae and animals that live in the ocean. They are eaten by many other animals.

predator animal that eats other animals. A shark is a predator of sea lions.

prey animal that gets eaten by other animals. A sea lion is one type of prey that sharks eat.

producer living thing that makes its own food. Algae are producers.

Want to Know More?

There's a lot of information out there about sharks and other ocean animals. Check these out:

Books

- Baldwin, Carol. *Sharks*. Chicago: Heinemann Library, 2003.
- Lynch, Emma. *Ocean Food Chains*. Chicago: Heinemann Library, 2005
- Markle, Sandra. *Great White Sharks*. Minneapolis: Carolhoda Books, 2004.
- Solway, Andrew. *Killer Fish*. Chicago: Heinemann Library, 2005.

Websites

- http://www.sdnhm.org/kids/sharks
  Want to learn more about sharks? Check out this cool website sponsored by the San Diego Natural History Museum.

Movies and DVDs

Get to know the shark's underwater world by watching a DVD of *The Blue Planet*. This nature film took five years to make. It shows parts of the ocean never seen before.

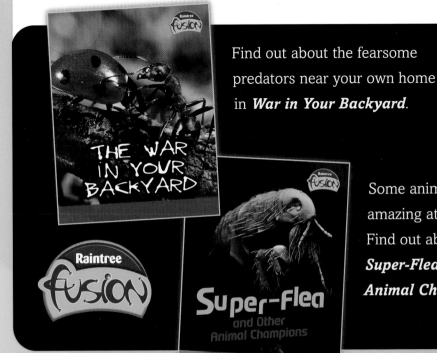

Find out about the fearsome predators near your own home in *War in Your Backyard*.

Some animals have amazing athletic abilities. Find out about these in *Super-Flea and Other Animal Champions*.

Index